Everybody's Favorite Series

EASY
PIANO PIECES
FOR
CHILDREN

Order No. AM1011439

Compiled and edited by Lisa Cox, Sam Lung and Andrew Skirrow.
Music engraved and processed by Camden Music Services.
Front cover illustration re-drawn by Sergio Sandoval.

Printed in the UK.

ISBN: 978-1-7855-8236-3

HAL•LEONARD®

Visit Hal Leonard Online at
www.halleonard.com

Contact us:
Hal Leonard
7777 West Bluemound Road
Milwaukee, WI 53213
Email: info@halleonard.com

In Europe, contact:
Hal Leonard Europe Limited
42 Wigmore Street
Marylebone, London, W1U 2RY
Email: info@halleonardeurope.com

In Australia, contact:
Hal Leonard Australia Pty. Ltd.
4 Lentara Court
Cheltenham, Victoria, 3192 Australia
Email: info@halleonard.com.au

COMPOSERS' INDEX

CONTENTS

The selections in this volume have been carefully selected
and edited with the beginner pianist in mind.
Each piece has been graded with stars to indicate difficulty,
beginning with Level 1 (★) and progressing through
to Level 4 (★★). Some students may progress quickly through
the early pages and so any skipped pieces can be later used
to refresh basic technique, or even as sight-reading practice.

Editorial markings have been included to introduce
the student to a number of techniques, and a glossary
of these symbols can be found at the end of this book.
Fingering has been suggested where appropriate, though the
student should always defer to the guidance of their teacher.

Cradle Song

Eduard Horak
1838–1893

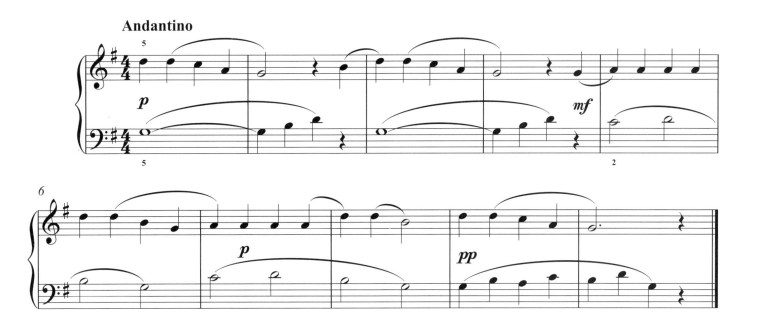

Gavotte

Georg Philipp Telemann
1681–1767

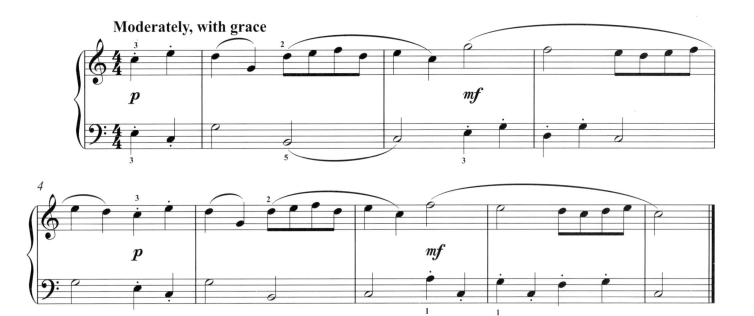

The Cranes Are Flying

Anton Arensky
1861–1906

Frolic

Daniel Gottlob Türk
1750–1813

Ode To Joy

Ludwig van Beethoven
1770–1827

Allegro assai

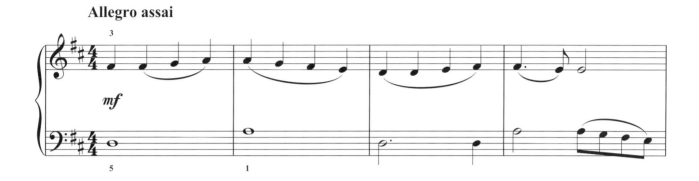

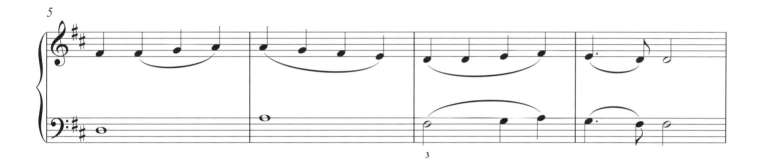

Gavotta

James Hook
1746–1827

Andantino

Greensleeves

Traditional

Briskly, in 1

Moonlight Sonata

Ludwig van Beethoven
1770–1827

Adagio sostenuto

rit.

Là ci darem la mano

from Don Giovanni

Wolfgang Amadeus Mozart
1756–1791

Moderato

Entr'acte

from Rosamunde

Franz Schubert
1797–1828

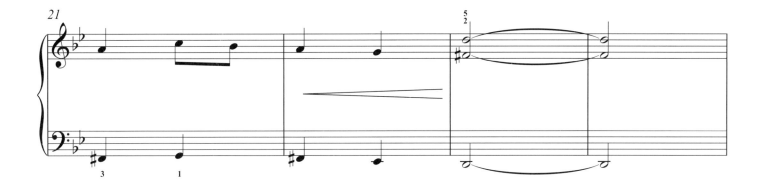

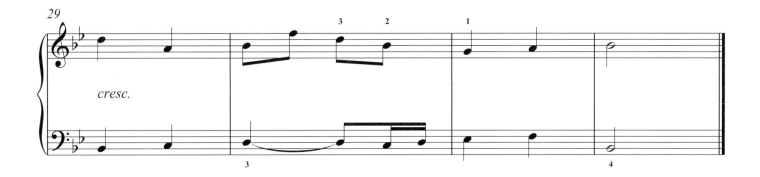

Minuet

Georg Philipp Telemann
1681–1767

Allegretto

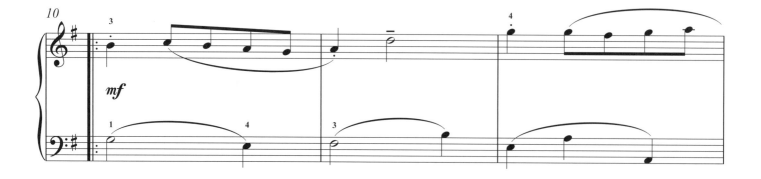

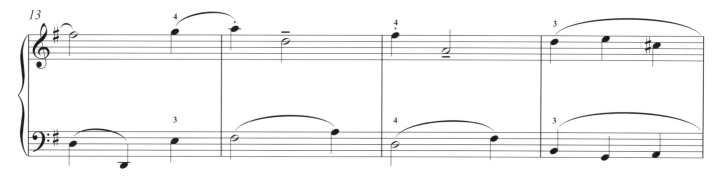

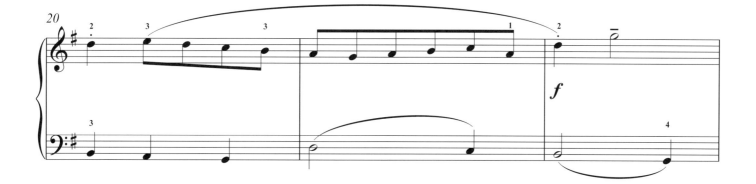

Jupiter
from The Planets

Gustav Holst
1874–1934

Andante maestoso

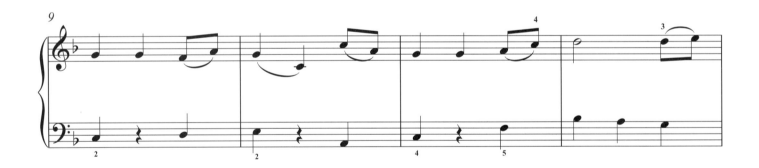

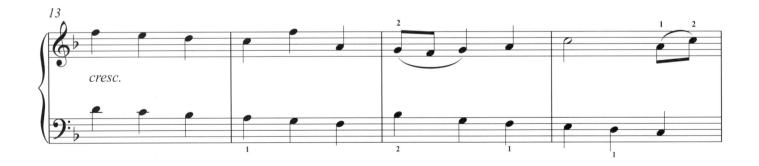

Panis Angelicus

César Franck
1822–1890

Poco lento

To Coda

D.C. al Coda

Coda

Quadrille

Joseph Haydn
1732–1809

Allegretto

The Harmonious Blacksmith

George Frideric Handel
1685–1759

Sweet As Sugar

No.1 *from* For Children, Vol. 1

Béla Bartók
1881–1945

Gavotte

George Frideric Handel
1685–1759

Andante

Minuet in G major

Johann Sebastian Bach
1685–1750

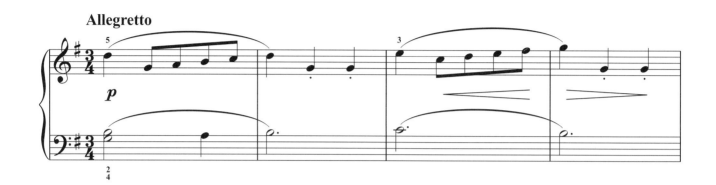

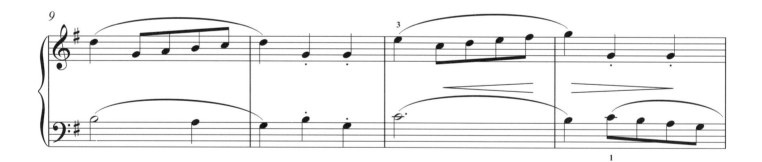

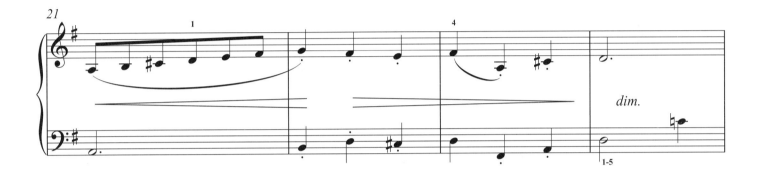

Minuet in F major

K. 2

Wolfgang Amadeus Mozart
1756–1791

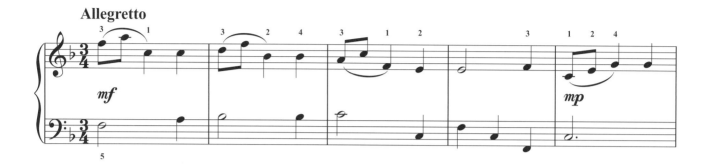

The Dancing Master

Daniel Gottlob Türk
1750–1813

Allegro moderato

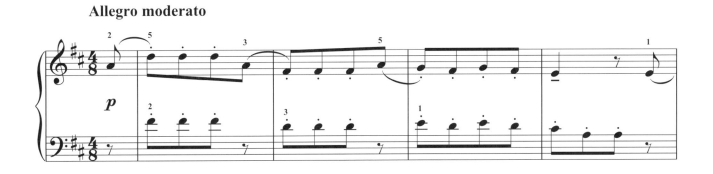

Short Canon

Konrad Max Kunz
1812–1875

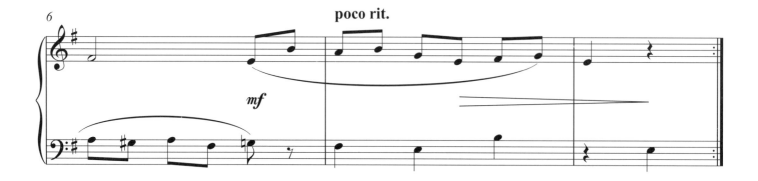

Russian Folk Song

Ludwig van Beethoven
1770–1827

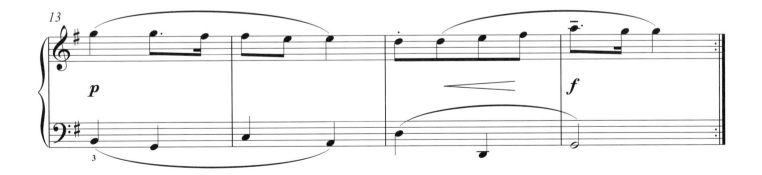

Hungarian Dance No. 5

Johannes Brahms
1833–1897

Allegro ♩ = 108

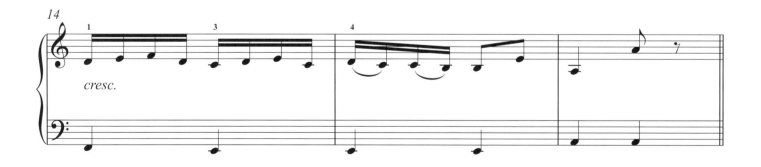

Soft Tears

No. 4 *from* For Children, Vol. 1

Béla Bartók
1881–1945

Autumn

from The Four Seasons

Antonio Vivaldi
1678–1741

Allegro

J'ai perdu mon Eurydice

from Orfeo ed Euridice

Christoph Willibald Gluck
1714 –1787

Andante con moto

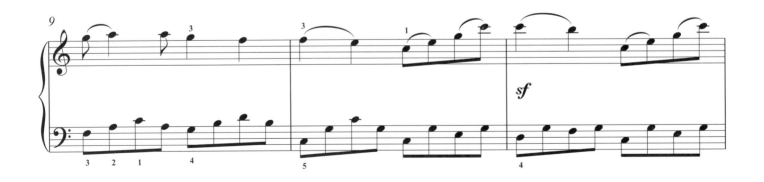

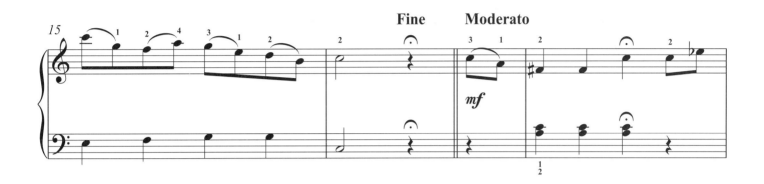

Fine **Moderato**

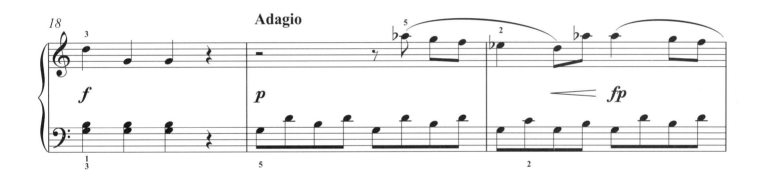

Adagio

D.C. al Fine

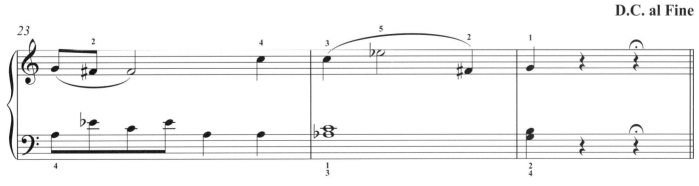

Trumpet Voluntary

Jeremiah Clarke
1674–1707

Andante maestoso

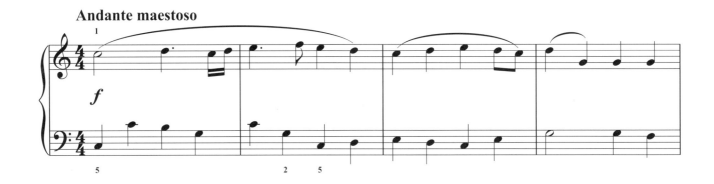

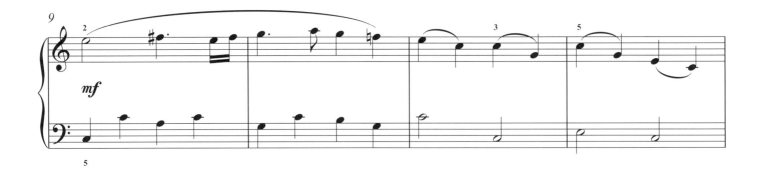

The Swan

from Carnival Of The Animals

Camille Saint-Saëns
1835–1921

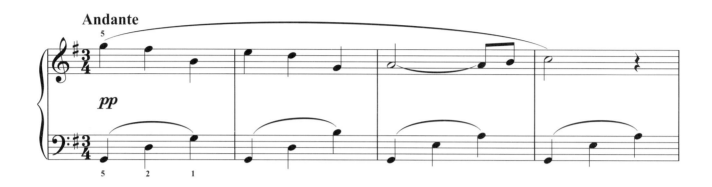

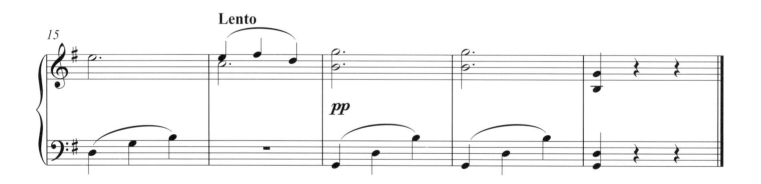

A Farewell

Henry Purcell
1659–1695

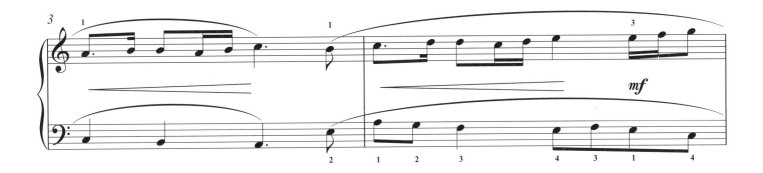

King William's March

Jeremiah Clarke
1674–1707

Tempo di marche

Danse Galante

Georg Philipp Telemann
1681–1767

Vivo

Bagatelle

Anton Diabelli
1781–1858

Allegretto

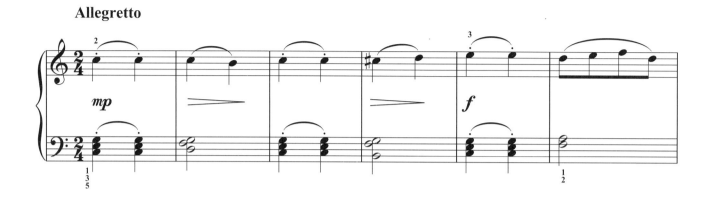

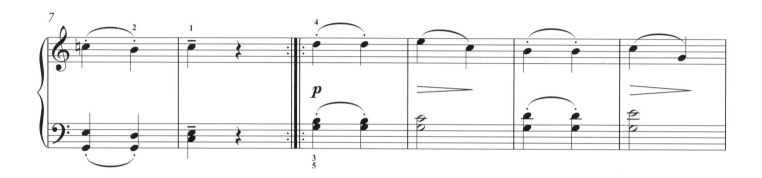

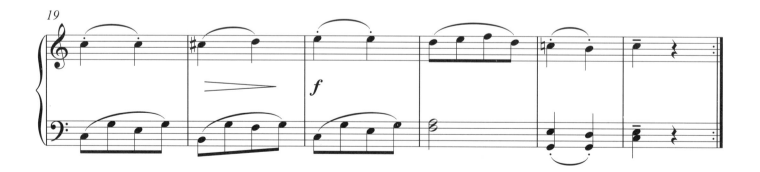

The Hunter's Song

Cornelius Gurlitt
1820–1901

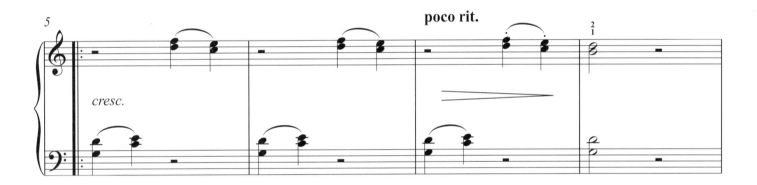

Clarinet Concerto

Adagio

Wolfgang Amadeus Mozart
1756–1791

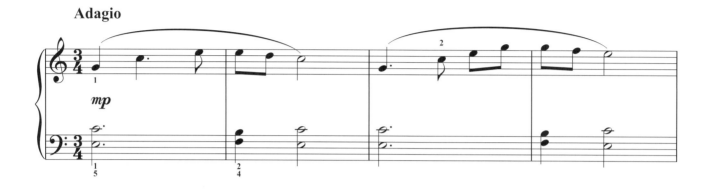

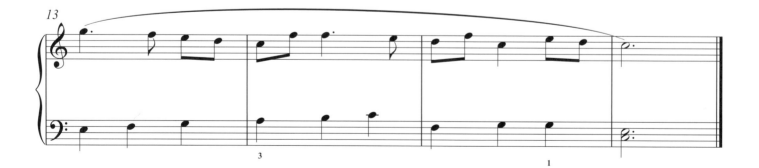

Walking

Anton Diabelli
1781–1858

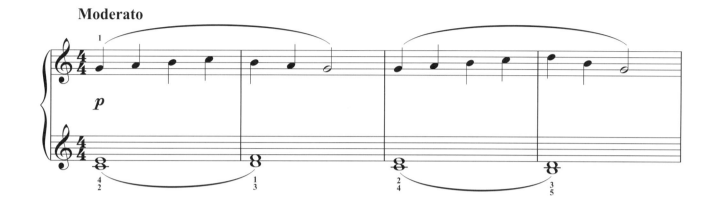

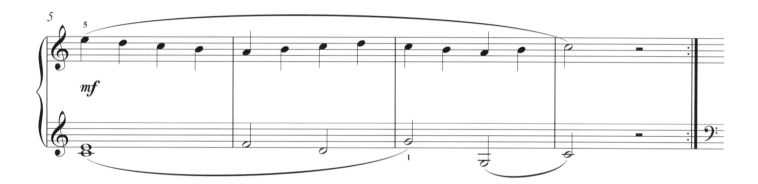

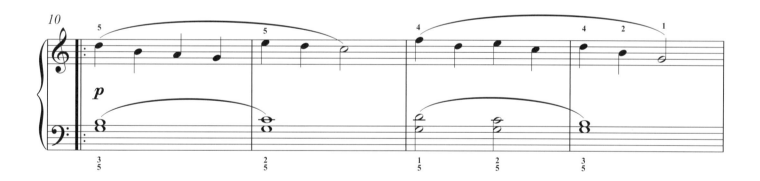

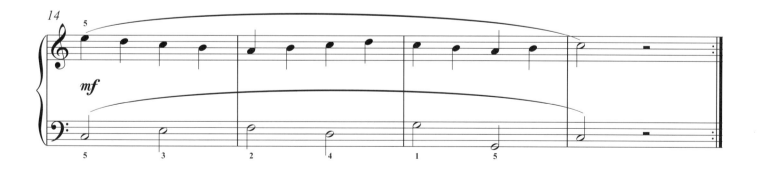

See The Conquering Hero Comes

from Judas Maccabaeus

George Frideric Handel
1685–1759

Majestically

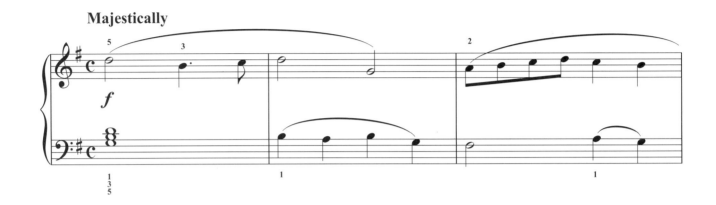

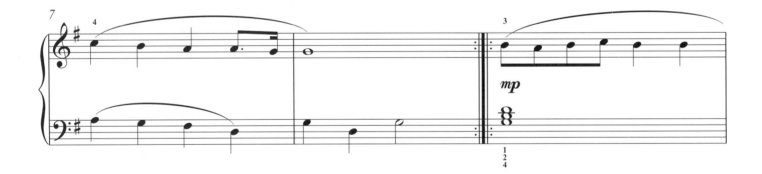

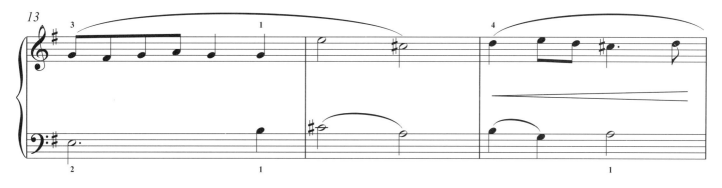

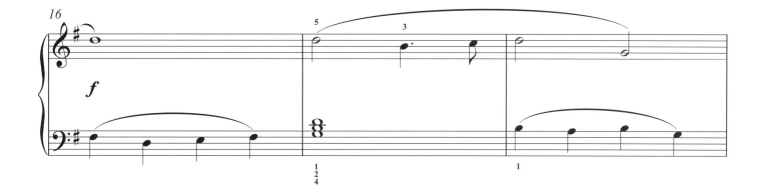

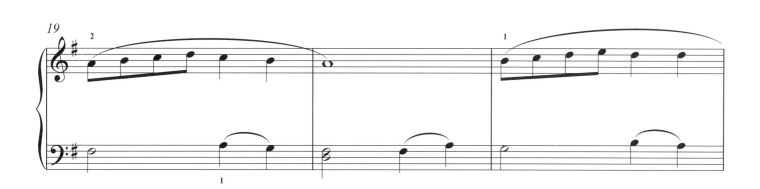

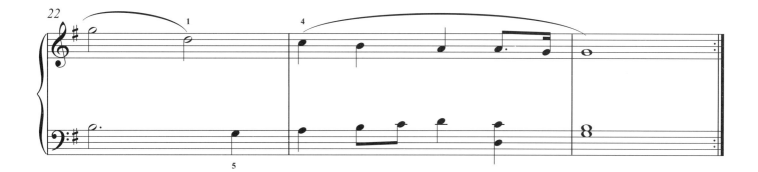

William Tell Overture

Gioachino Rossini
1792–1868

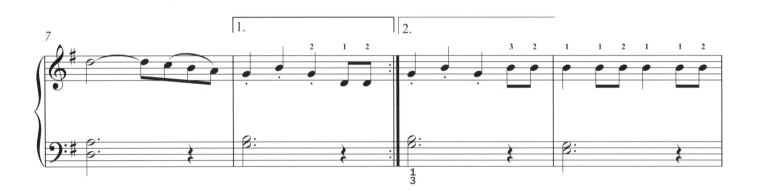

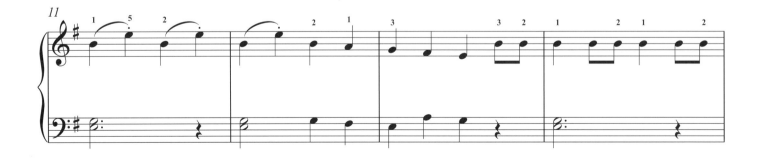

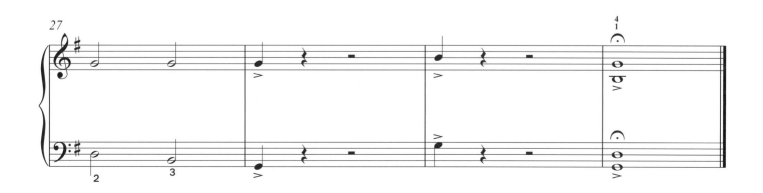

Minuet

Leopold Mozart
1719–1787

Andantino grazioso

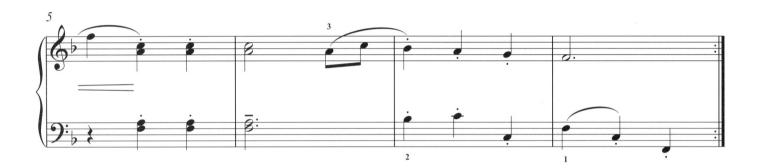

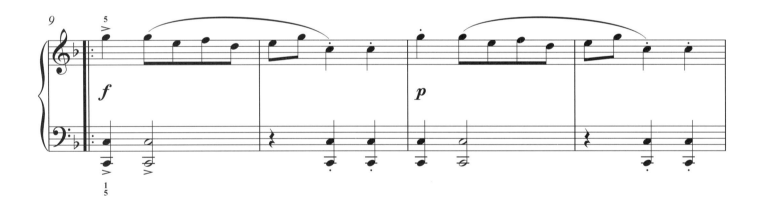

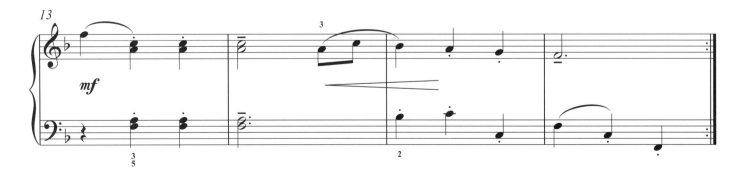

Fanfare Minuet

William Duncombe
1738–1818

Moderato

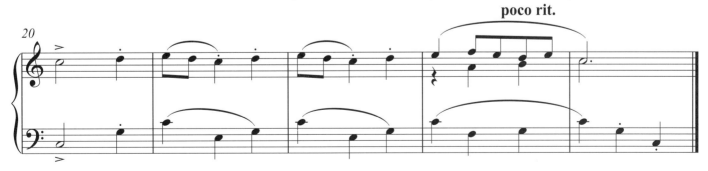

Surprise Symphony

Theme

Joseph Haydn
1732–1809

Prelude

Henry Purcell
1659–1695

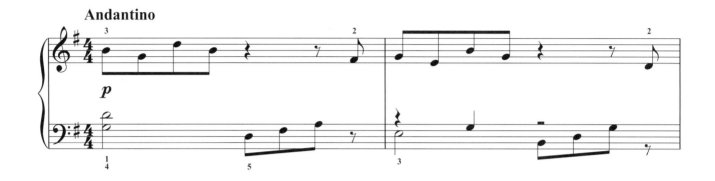

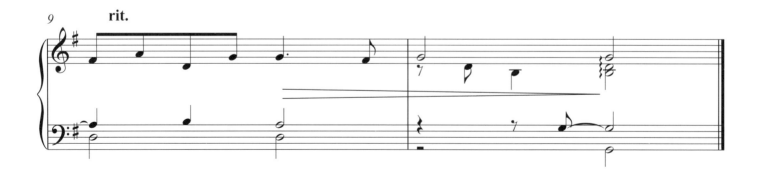

German Dance

Joseph Haydn
1732–1809

Allegretto

Für Elise

Ludwig van Beethoven
1770–1827

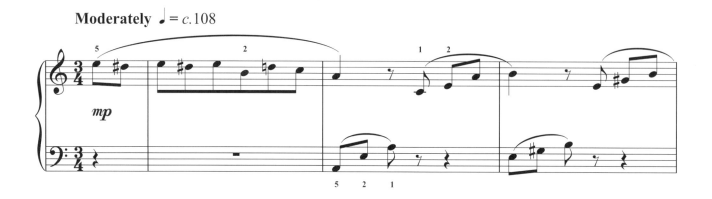

Brindisi

from La Traviata

Giuseppe Verdi
1813–1901

Lullaby

Johannes Brahms
1833–1897

Zart bewegt

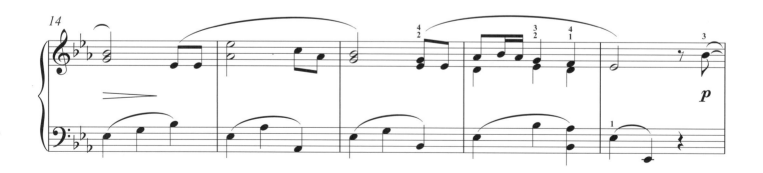

langsamer

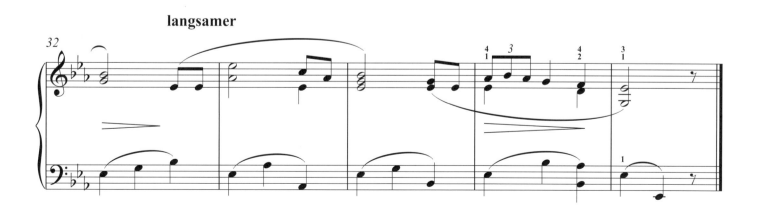

The Can-Can

from Orpheus In The Underworld

Jacques Offenbach
1819–1880

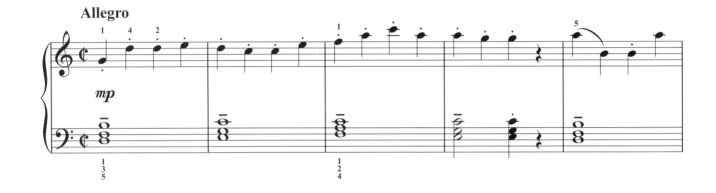

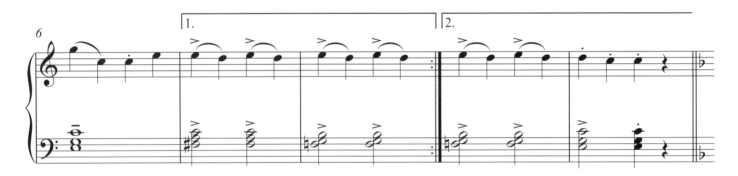

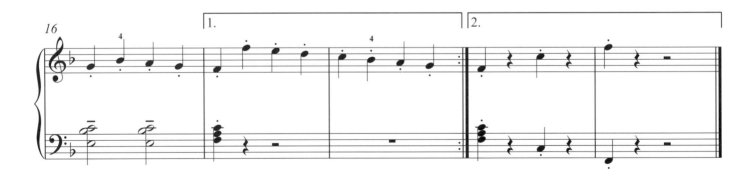

Burleske

Leopold Mozart
1719–1787

Dance Of The Sylphs

Hector Berlioz
1803–1869

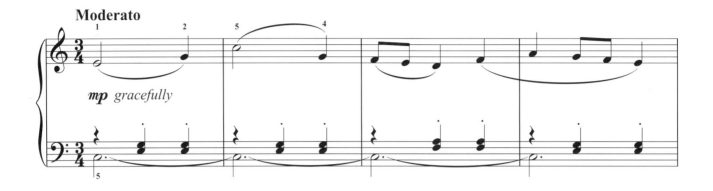

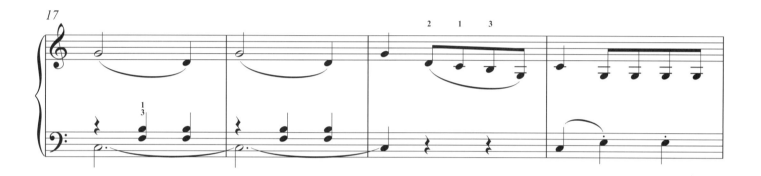

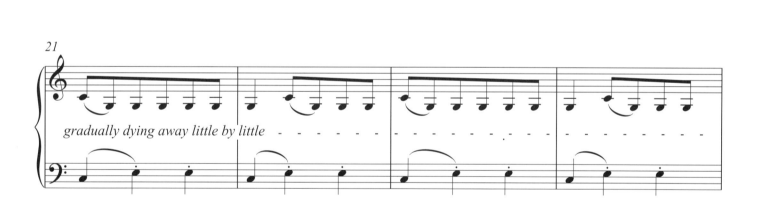

gradually dying away little by little - - - - - - - - - -

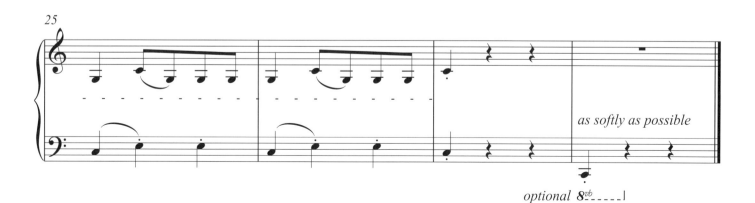

as softly as possible

optional 8vb - - - - - |

Minuet in G minor

Johann Sebastian Bach
1685–1750

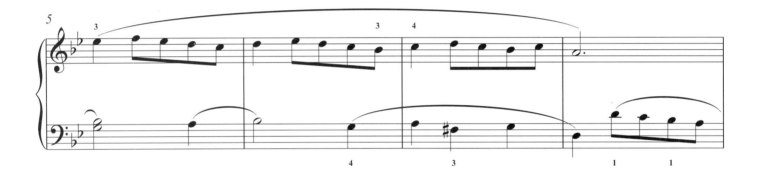

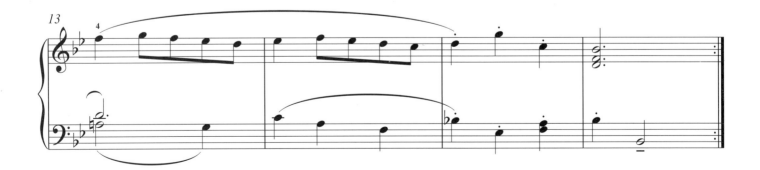

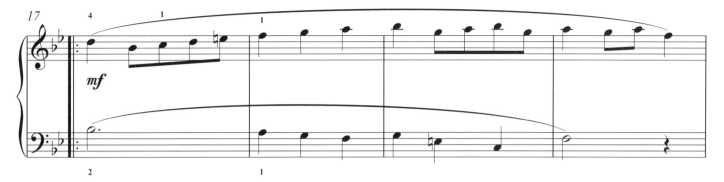

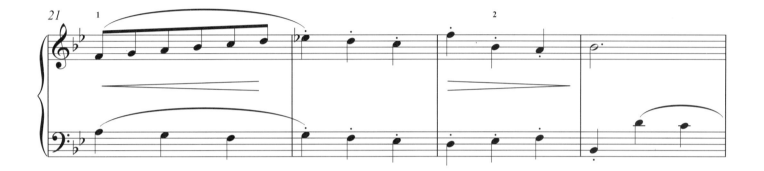

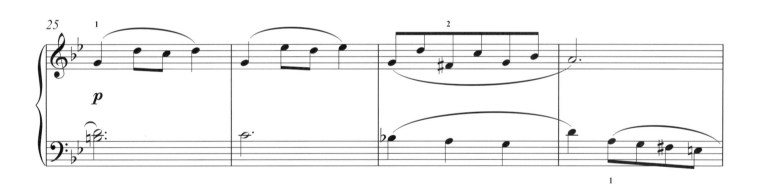

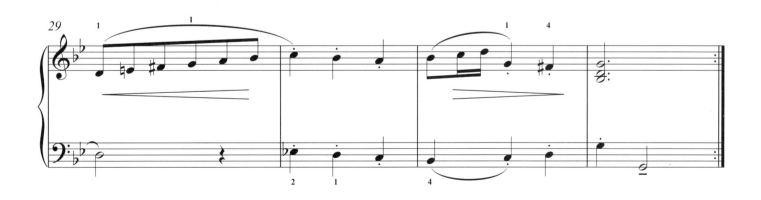

Melody

from Album For The Young

Robert Schumann
1810–1856

Moderato

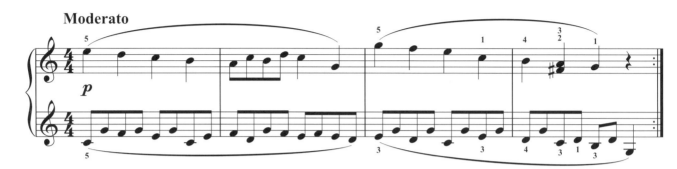

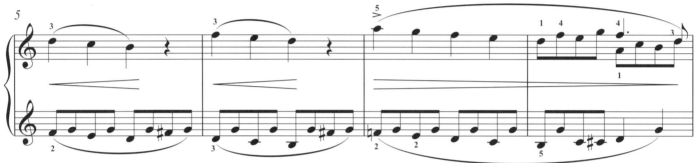

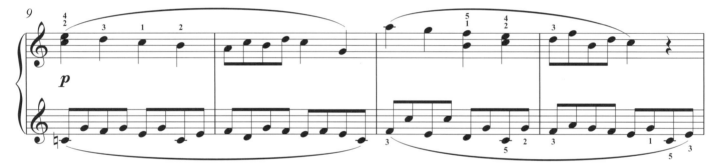

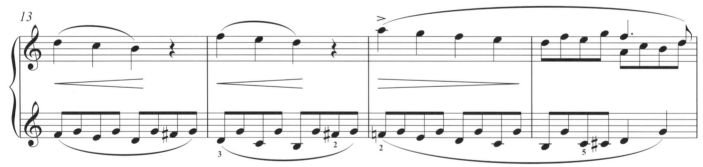

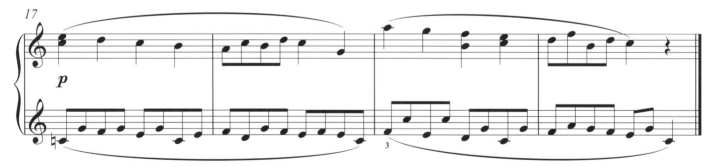

Little Scherzo

Carl Philipp Emanuel Bach
1714–1788

Allegretto

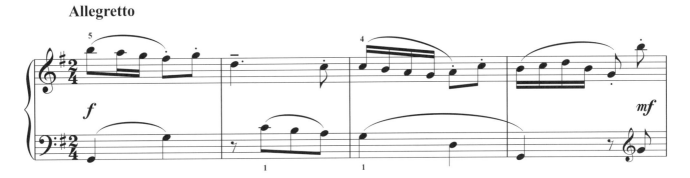

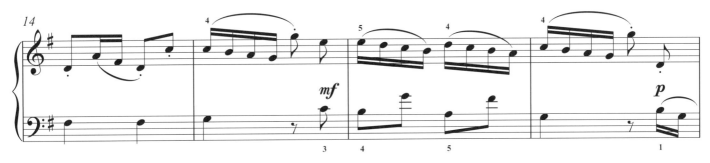

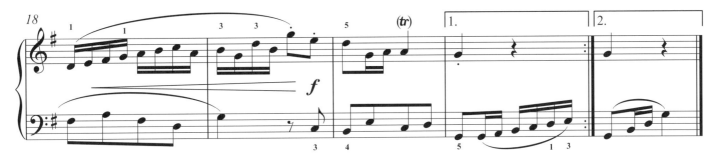

Little Piece

from Album For The Young

Robert Schumann
1810–1856

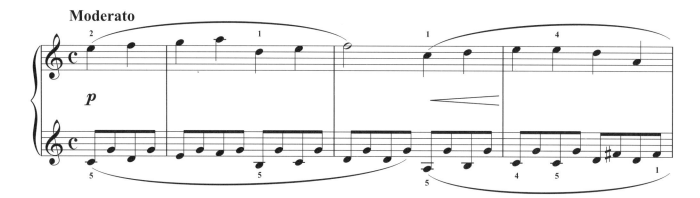

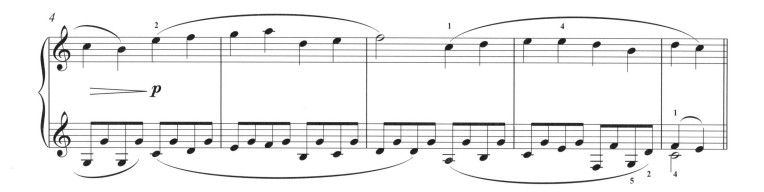

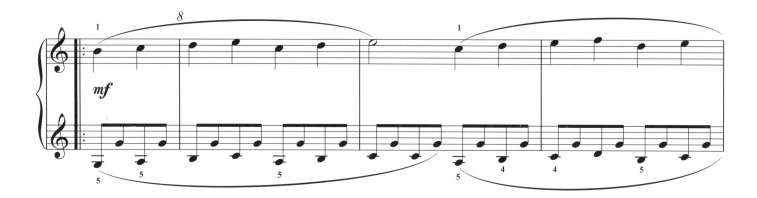

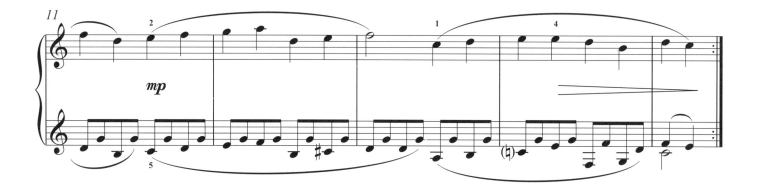

Ecossaise

Johann Nepomuk Hummel
1778–1837

Vivace

Prelude No. 1 in C major

Johann Sebastian Bach
1685–1750

Moderato e legato

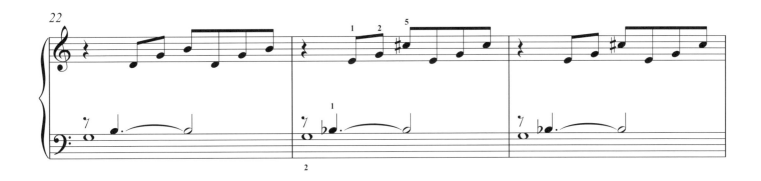

Ecossaise in G

Ludwig van Beethoven
1770–1827

Playful Dialogue

Johann Nepomuk Hummel
1778–1837

Moderato

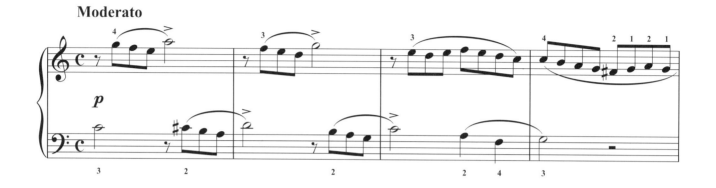

German Dance

Ludwig van Beethoven
1770–1827

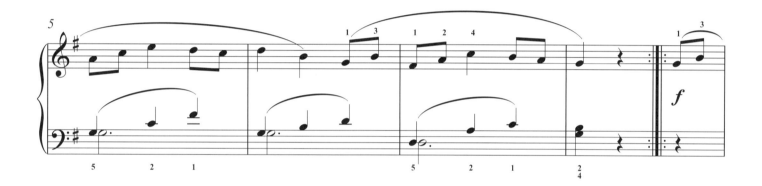

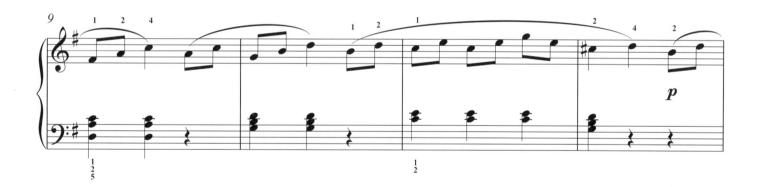

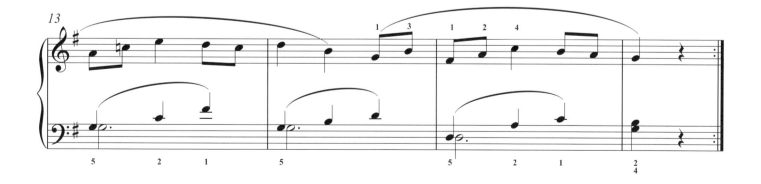

Farandole

from L'Arlésienne Suite

Georges Bizet
1838–1875

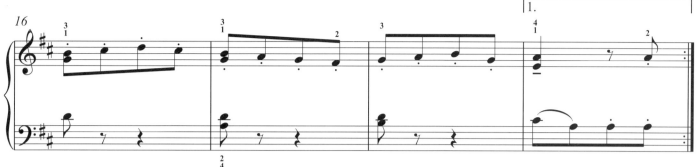

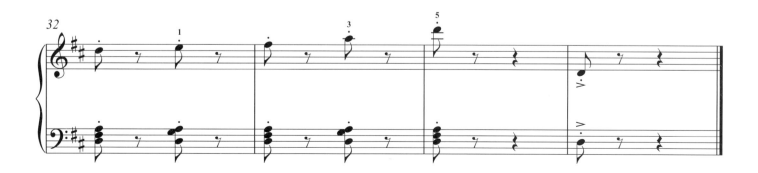

Méditation

from Thaïs

Jules Massenet
1842–1912

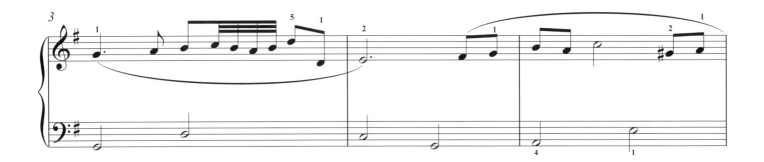

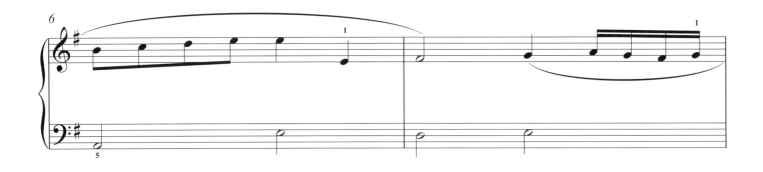

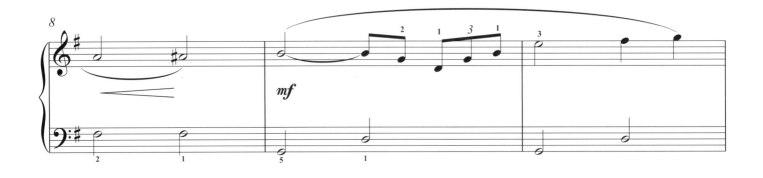

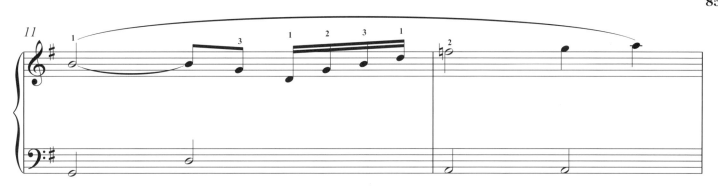

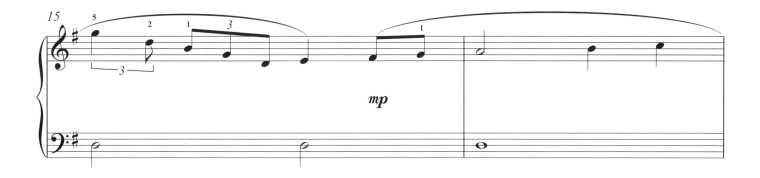

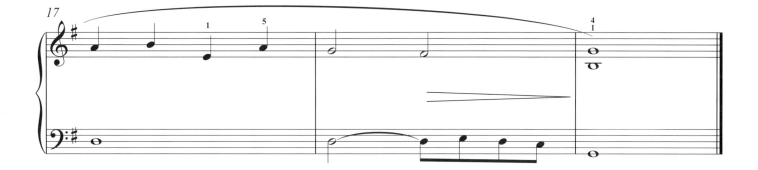

The Hiding Cuckoo

Robert Schumann
1810–1856

Scherzando

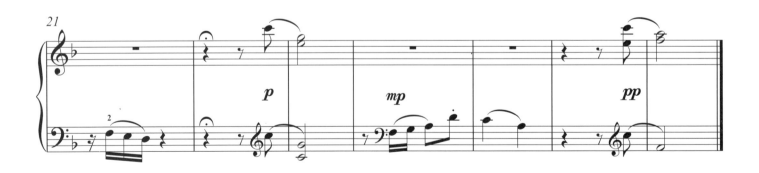

Hornpipe
from Water Music

George Frideric Handel
1685–1759

Brightly

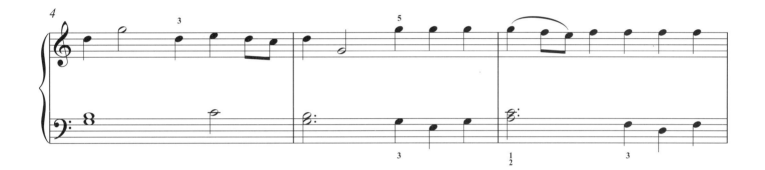

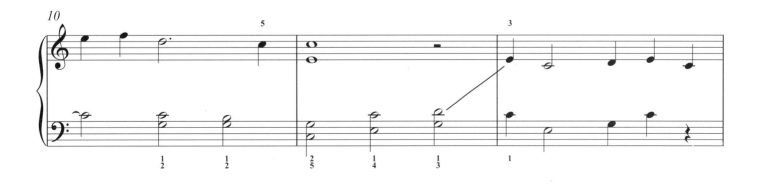

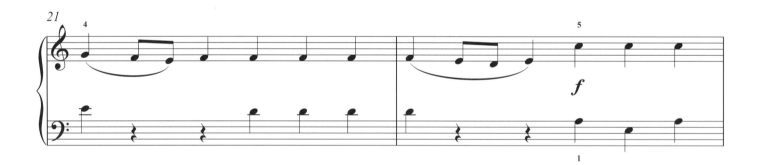

rall.

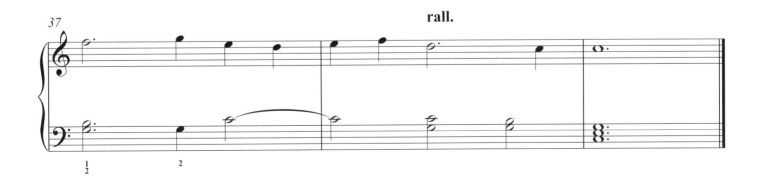

Scene Finale from Swan Lake

Pyotr Ilyich Tchaikovsky
1840–1893

Aylesford Piece

George Frideric Handel
1685–1759

Vivace

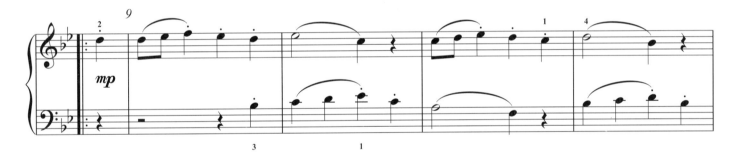

Largo

from Symphony No. 9 "From The New World"

Antonín Dvořák
1841–1904

Largo

Sarabande in D minor

George Frideric Handel
1685–1759

Gavotte

Daniel Gottlob Türk
1750–1813

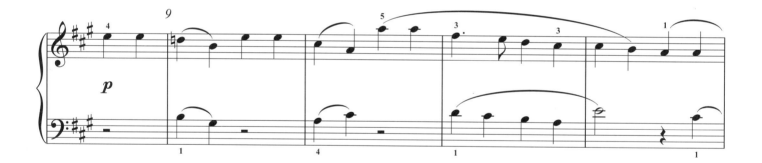

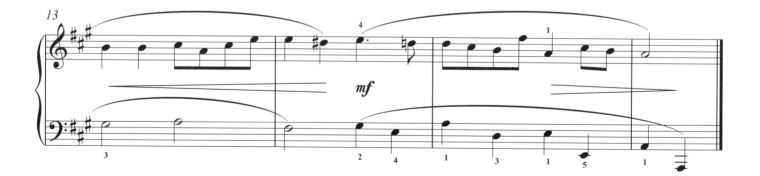

Children's Song

No.2 *from* For Children, Vol. 1

Béla Bartók
1881–1945

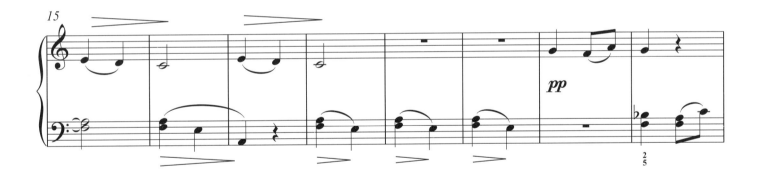

Former Friends

No.3 *from* For Children, Vol. 1

Béla Bartók
1881–1945

Eine Kleine Nachtmusik

Wolfgang Amadeus Mozart
1756–1791

Allegro

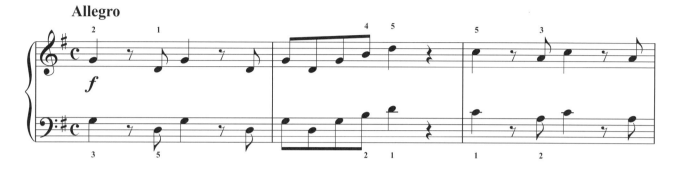

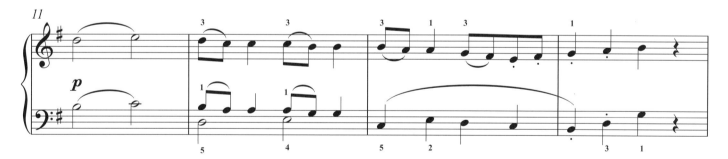

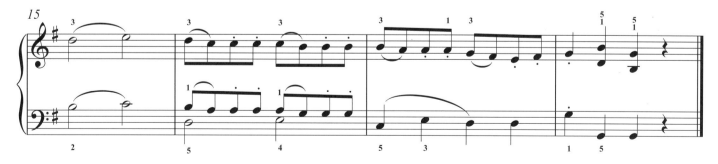

Bagatelle

Johann Nepomuk Hummel
1778–1837

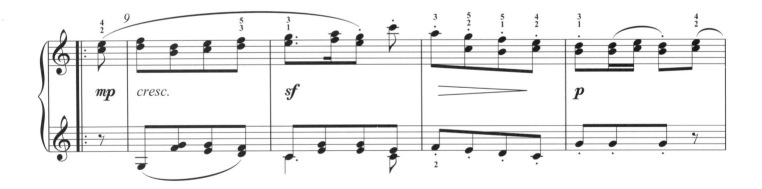

Minuet

K. 15c *from* London Notebook

Wolfgang Amadeus Mozart
1756–1791

Andante moderato

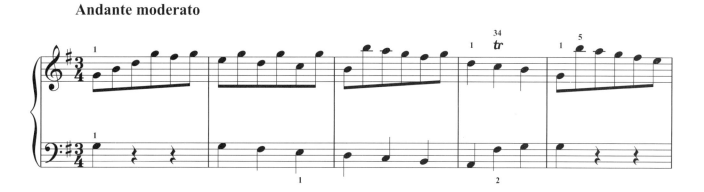

En Bateau

from Petite Suite

Claude Debussy
1862–1918

Andantino

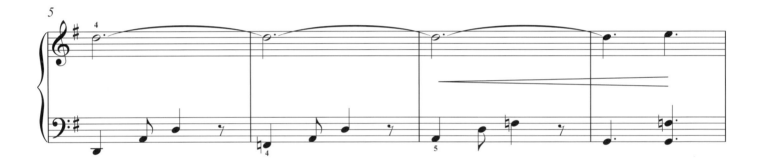

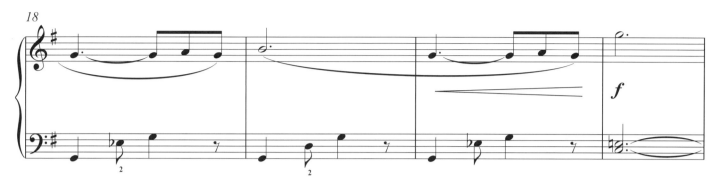

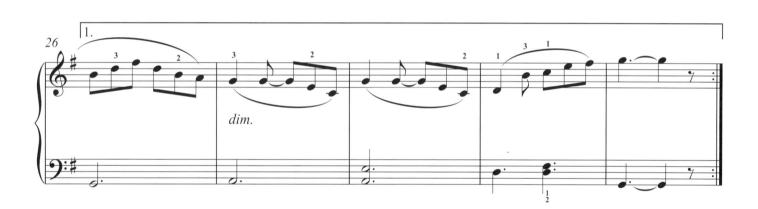

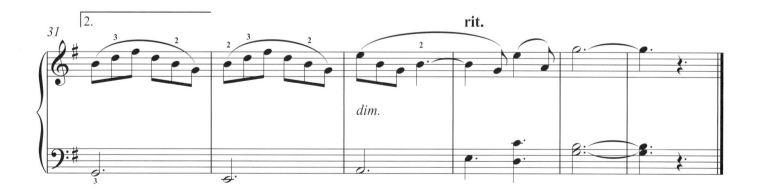

Gigue à l'Anglaise

Georg Philipp Telemann
1681–1767

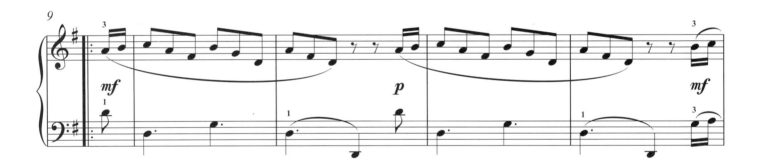

Dance Of The Sugar Plum Fairy

from The Nutcracker Suite

Pyotr Ilyich Tchaikovsky
1840–1893

Entrée

Leopold Mozart
1719–1787

Allegretto

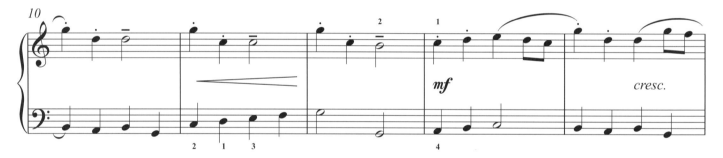

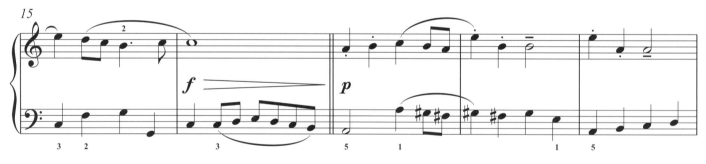

Symphony No. 104

Second Movement

Joseph Haydn
1732–1809

Moderato

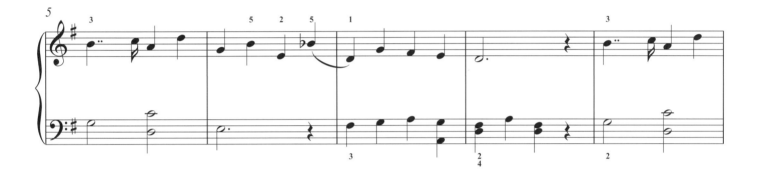

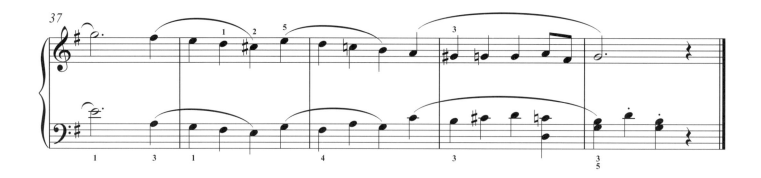

Serenade

Daniel Gottlob Türk
1750–1813

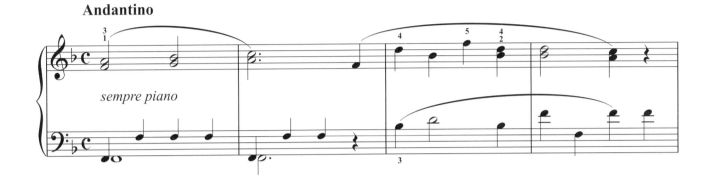

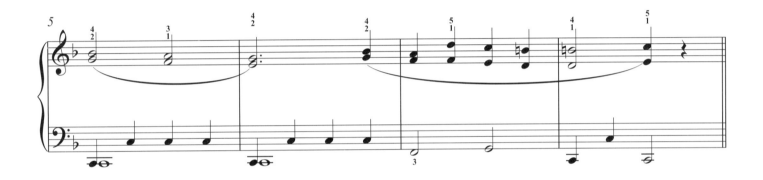

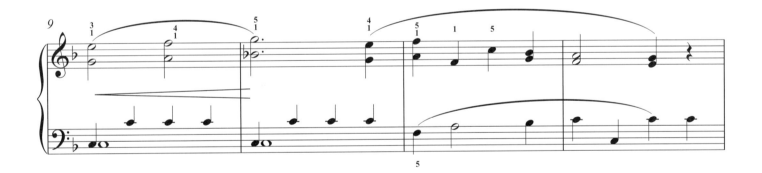

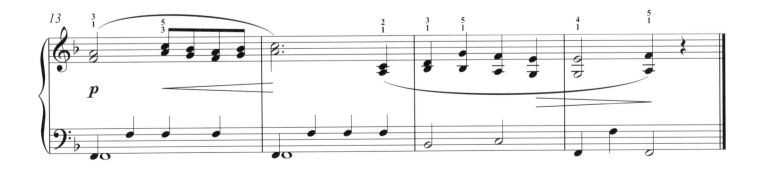

Minuet

K. 315a

Wolfgang Amadeus Mozart
1756–1791

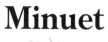

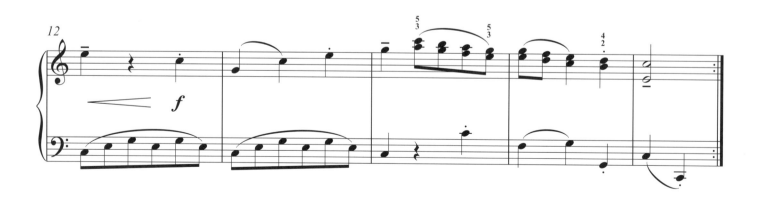

The Ruins Of Athens

Ludwig van Beethoven
1770–1827

Bright tempo

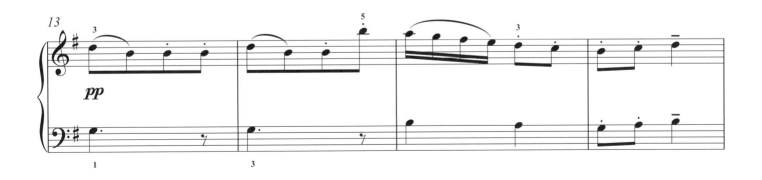

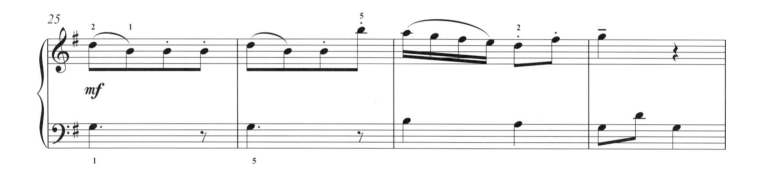

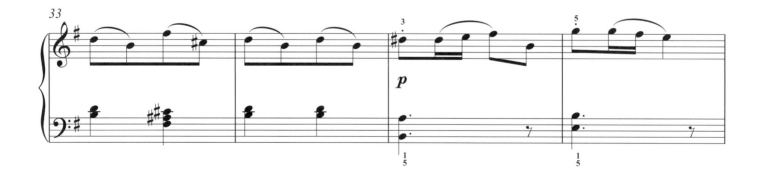

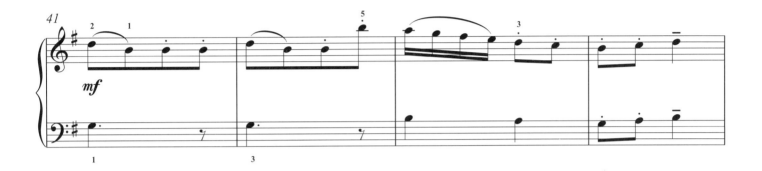

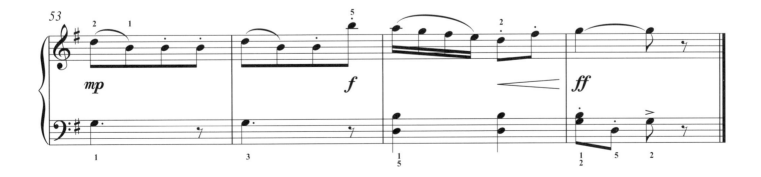

Hungarian Dance No. 6

Johannes Brahms
1833–1897

Tempo primo

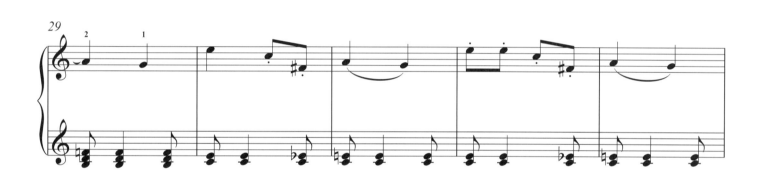

Nocturne in E♭

Op. 9, No. 2

Frédéric Chopin
1810–1849

Andante

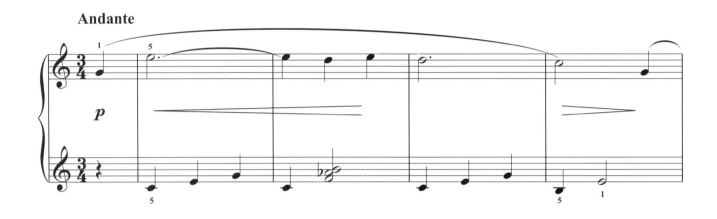

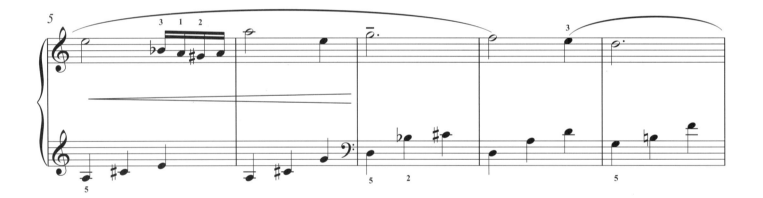

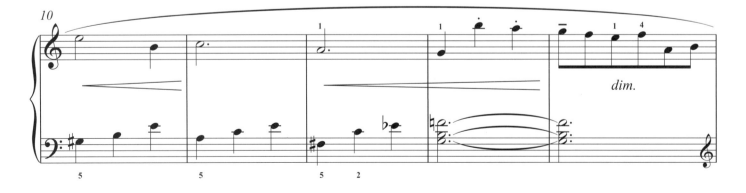

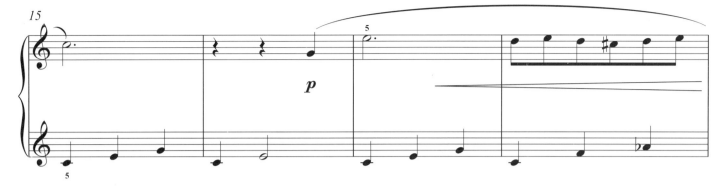

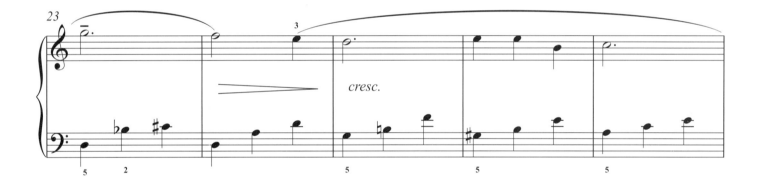

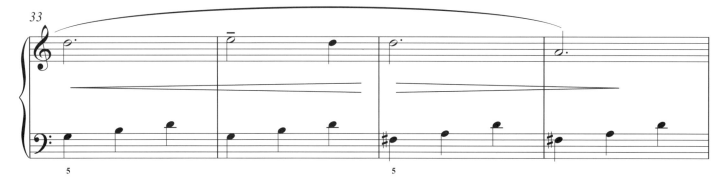

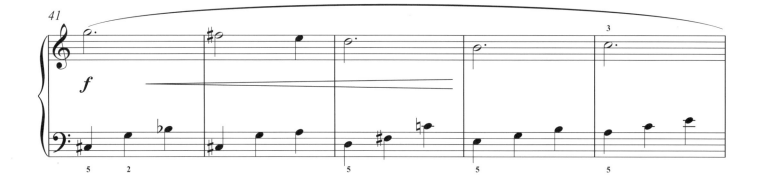

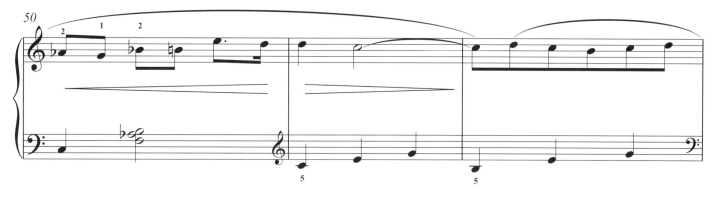

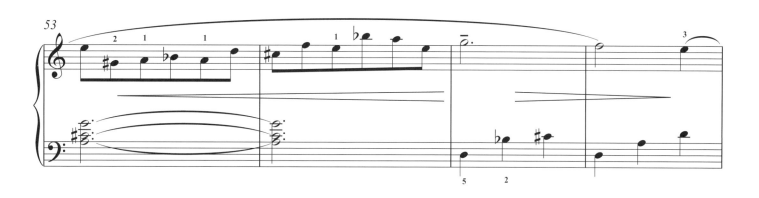

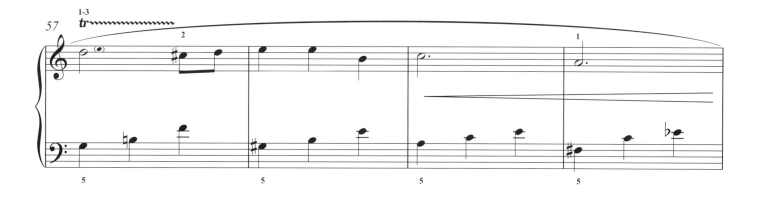

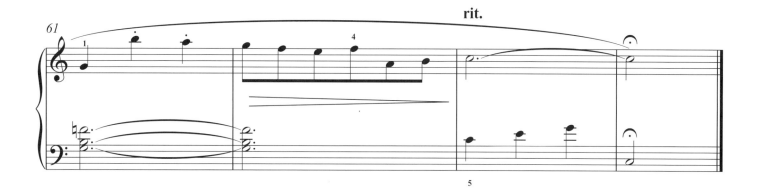

Largo

from Xerxes

George Frideric Handel
1685–1759

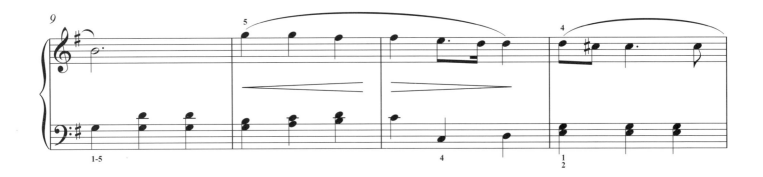

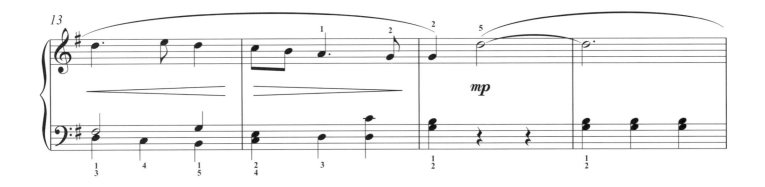

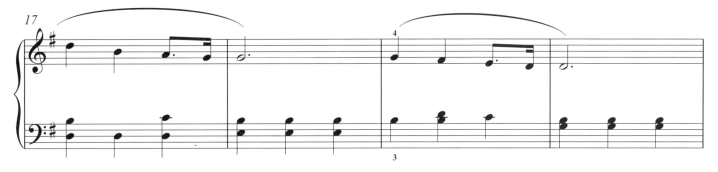

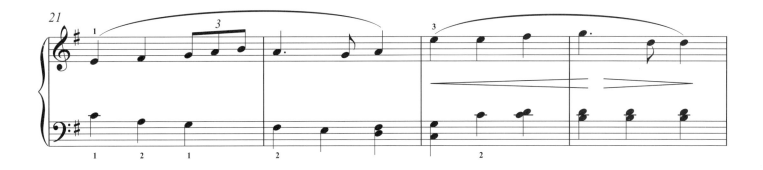

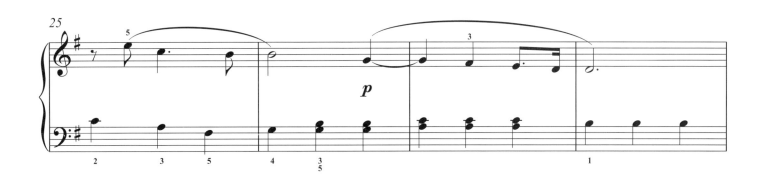

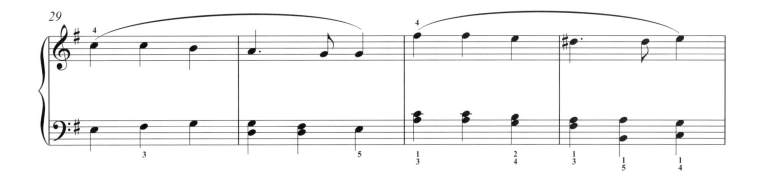

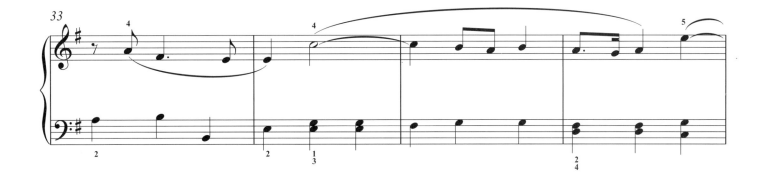

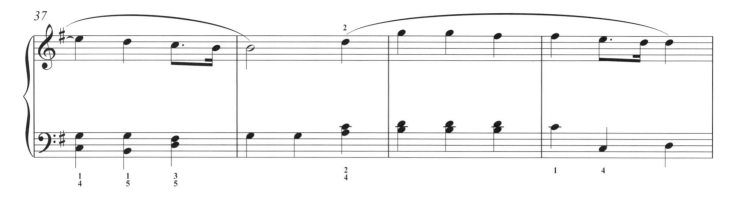

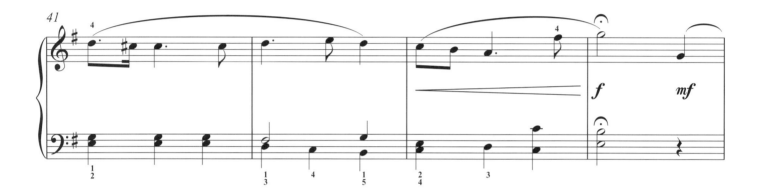

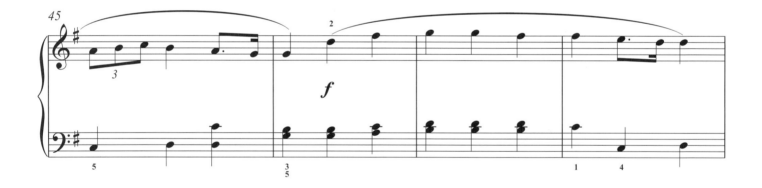

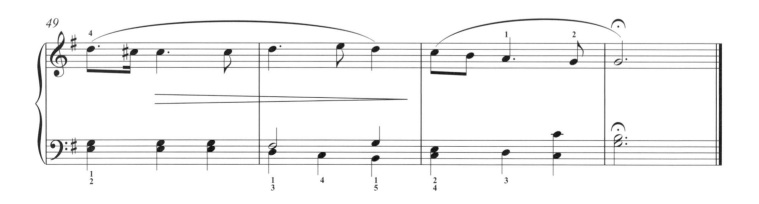

Waltz from Swan Lake

Pyotr Ilyich Tchaikovsky
1840–1893

Tempo di valse

Bourée

from Music For The Royal Fireworks

George Frideric Handel
1685–1759

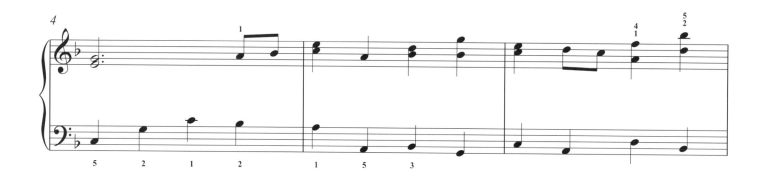

Pastorale

Carl Philipp Emanuel Bach
1714–1788

Andantino cantabile

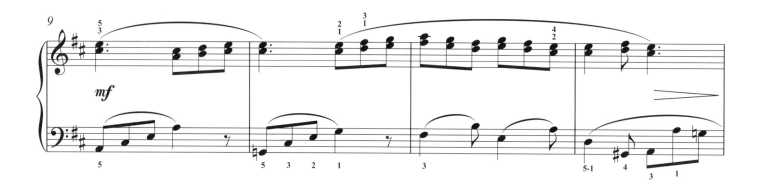

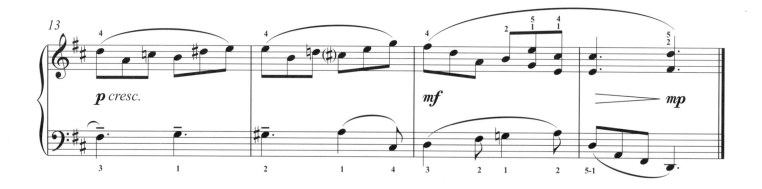

Chanson de Matin

Edward Elgar
1857–1934

Allegretto

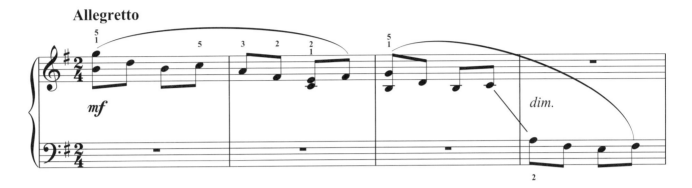

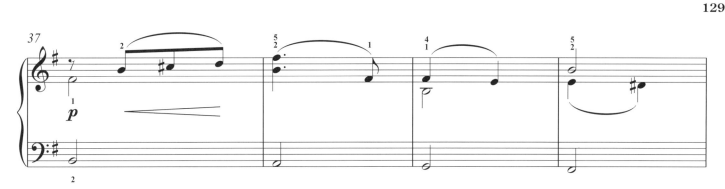

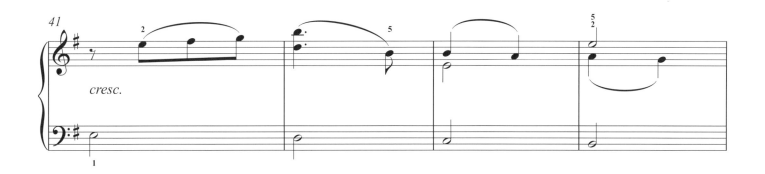

Air On The G String

Johann Sebastian Bach
1685–1750

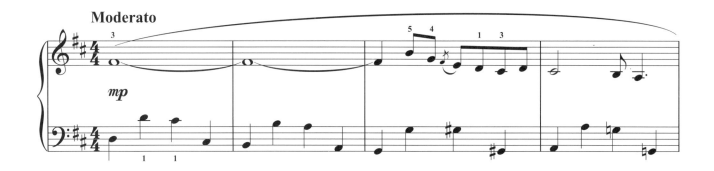

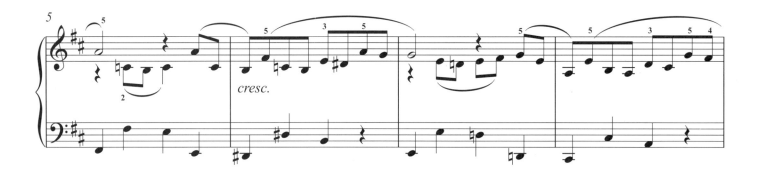

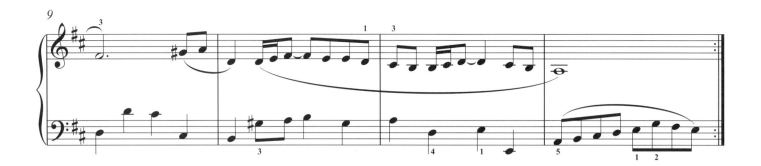

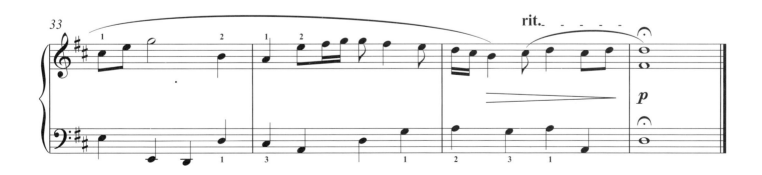

Gypsy Dance

Joseph Haydn
1732–1809

Allegro moderato

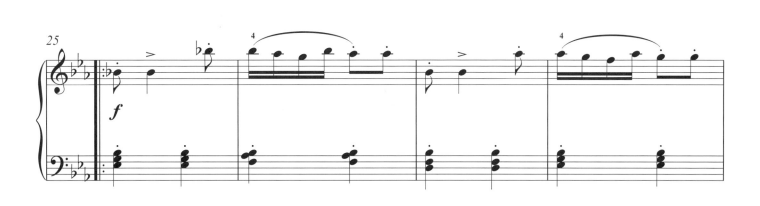

The Arrival Of The Queen Of Sheba

from Solomon

George Frideric Handel
1685–1759

Allegro

Serenade

from String Quartet Op. 3, No. 5

Joseph Haydn
1732–1809

Andante cantabile

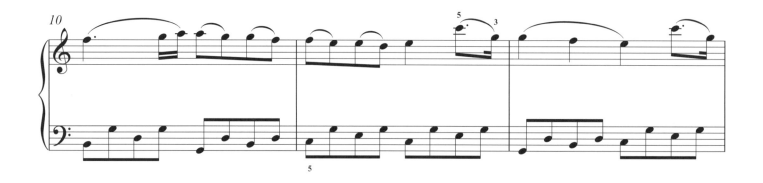

Puppet's Complaint

César Franck
1822–1890

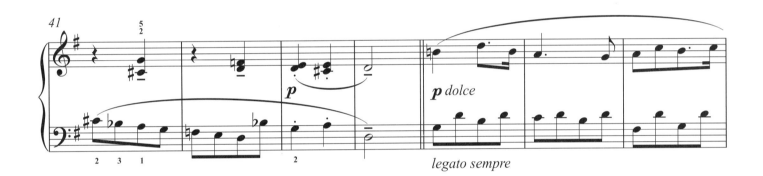

Morning

from Peer Gynt

Edvard Grieg
1843–1907

Allegretto pastorale

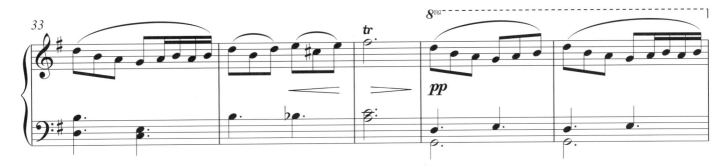

Spring Song

Wolfgang Amadeus Mozart
1756–1791

Allegretto giocoso

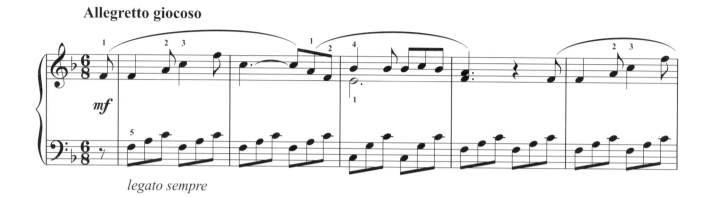

Soldier's March

from Album For The Young

Robert Schumann
1810–1856

Allegro

Waltz in A major

Franz Schubert
1797–1828

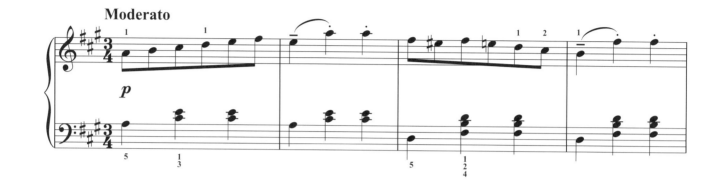

Prélude

Op. 2, No. 4

Georges Bizet
1838-1875

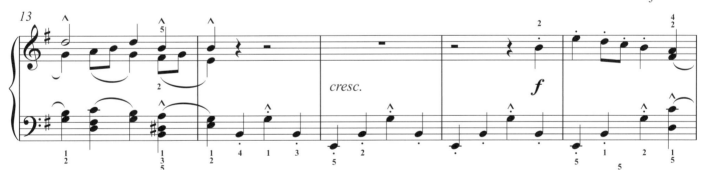

Salut d'Amour

Edward Elgar
1857–1934

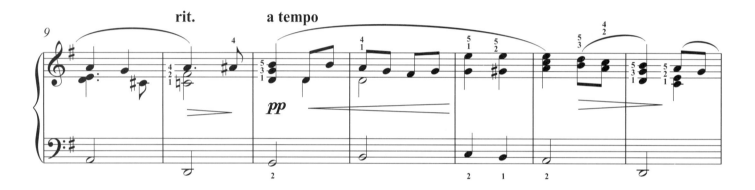

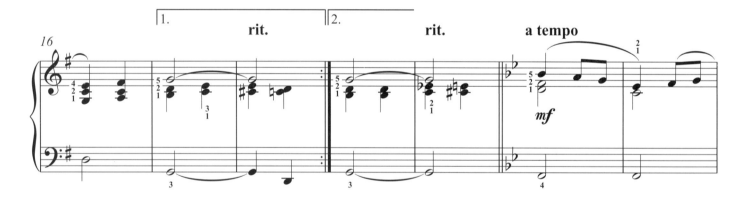

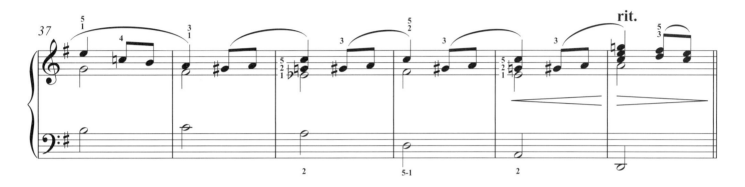

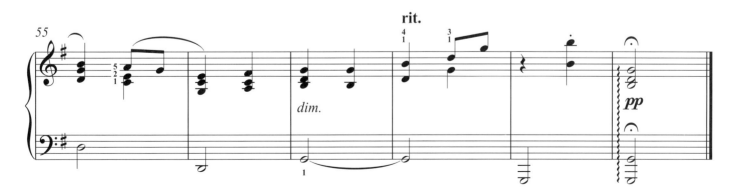

Habañera

from Carmen

Georges Bizet
1838-1875

Allegretto quasi andantino ♩ = 72

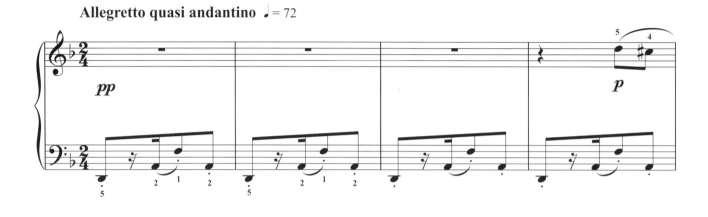

Sonata Facile

Wolfgang Amadeus Mozart
1756–1791

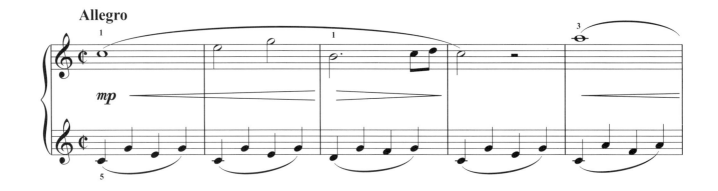

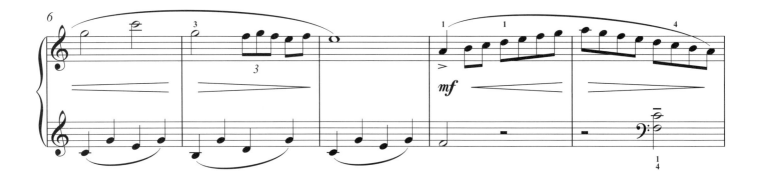

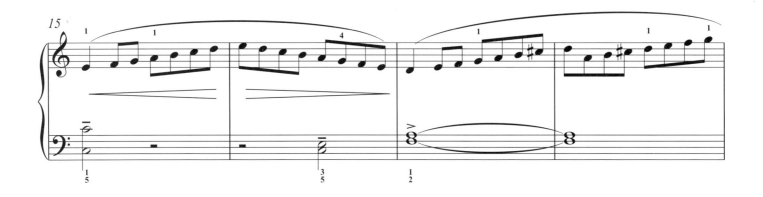

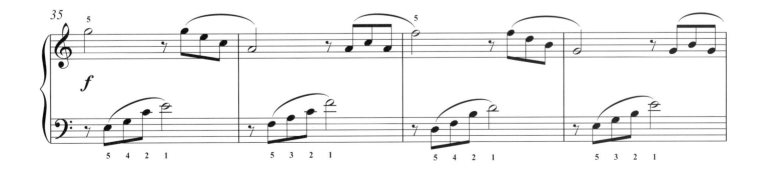

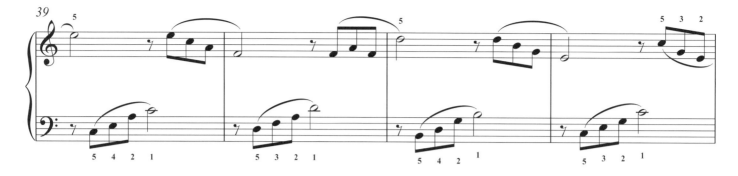

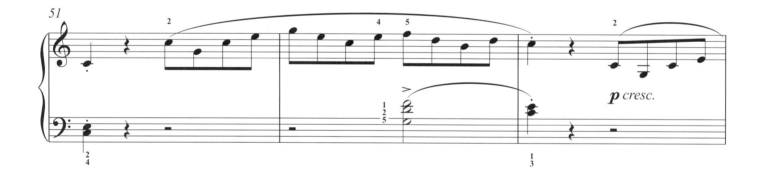

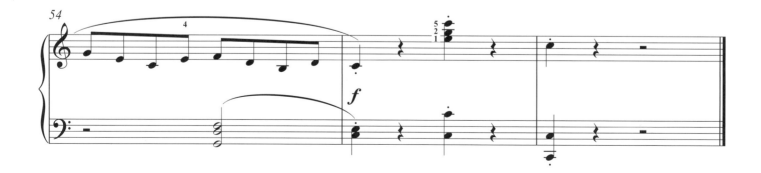

Humoresque No. 7

Antonín Dvořák
1841–1904

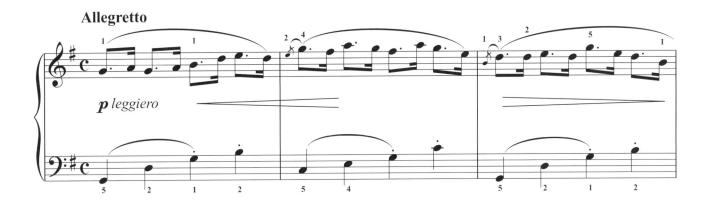

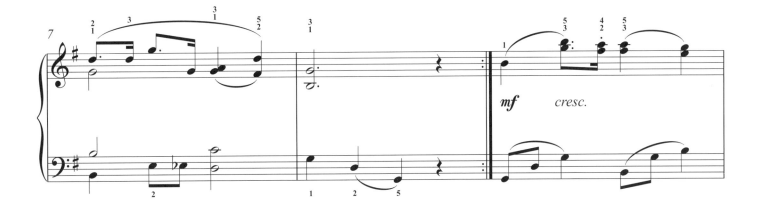

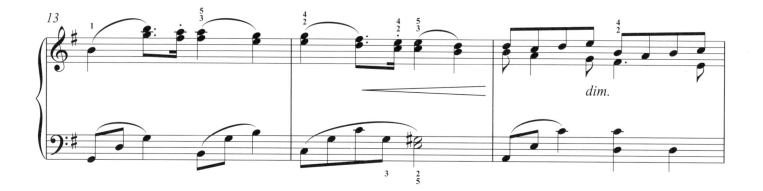

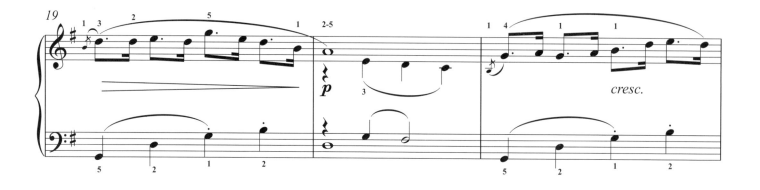

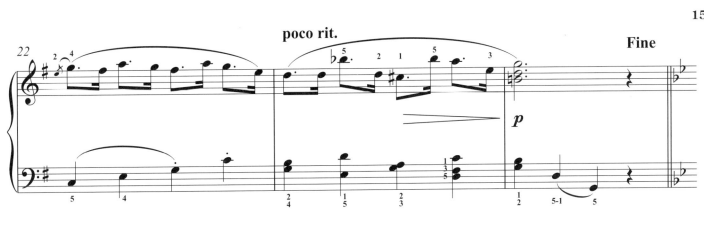

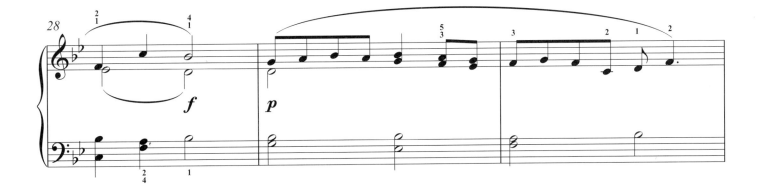

Raindrop Prelude

Frédéric Chopin
1810–1849

Sostenuto

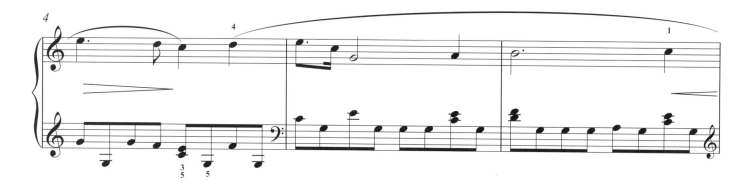

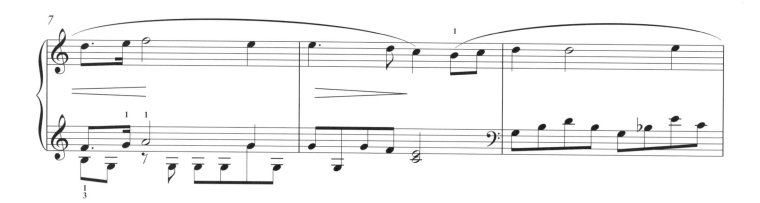

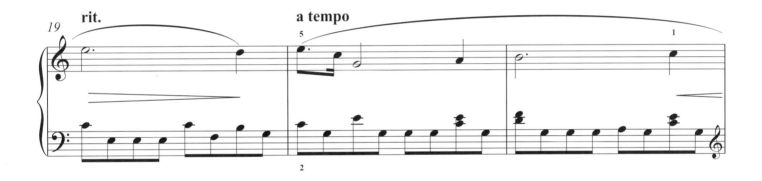

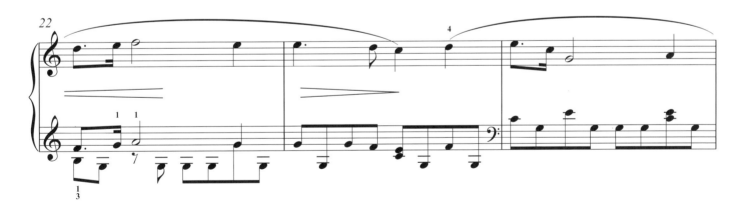

MUSIC SYMBOLS

ACCENTS AND ARTICULATIONS

Accent Marks

fz or **ffz**   **Forzando.** A strong, loud accent.

fp   **Forte piano.** A strong, loud accent which instantly diminishes to a soft volume.

sf, sz, or **sfz**   **Sforzando** (also **Sforzato**). A very strong, sudden, and loud accent.

sfp   **Sforzando piano.** A very strong, sudden, and loud accent which instantly diminishes to a soft volume

Notes marked with any of these accent signs are to be played with a strong accent and held for their full note value.

Slurs

A curved line connecting two or more notes indicates that they should be played smoothly.

Sometimes a slur is used with staccato markings to indicate that the notes be played halfway between staccato and legato—detached, yet somewhat smooth.

Staccato Marks

A dot above or below a note or chord indicates that it should be played with a light, crisp accent. A staccato note or chord receives less than half its indicated value.

A triangle above or below a note or chord also indicates staccato; usually with somewhat more stress.

Ties

The tie is similar in appearance to the slur. The tie indicates that two notes of the same pitch to be played as one note value.

When two or more ties are used in sequence, the note should be held for the combined value of all tied notes.

Phrase Mark

Like the slur, the *phrase mark* indicates that a passage be played in a smooth and connected manner. Each phrase of a piece is expressed as a distinctive musical idea, like a sentence.

DYNAMICS

Dynamic Marks

ppp	**Pianississimo**	*As soft as possible.*
pp	**Pianissimo**	Very soft
p	**Piano**	Soft
mp	**Mezzo piano**	Moderately soft
mf	**Mezzo forte**	Moderately loud
f	**Forte**	Loud
ff	**Fortissimo**	Very loud
fff	**Fortissississimo**	As loud as possible

Crescendo Mark

A gradual increase in volume is indicated by a *crescendo mark*.

Diminuendo Mark

A gradual decrease in volume is indicated by a diminuendo mark.

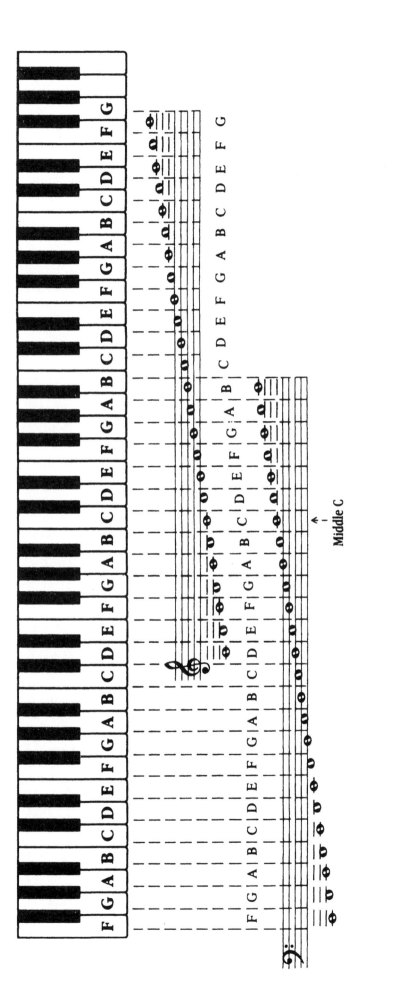

Easy Piano Pieces For Children

INDEX BY DIFFICULTY — TEACHER'S GUIDE